Ákaitsinikssiistsi

• • • • • • • • • • • • • • • • • •

Blackfoot
Stories of Old

D1596362

FIRST
NATIONS
LANGUAGE
READERS

BLACKFOOT

BRESCIA UNIVERSITY
COLLEGE LIBRARY

Ákaitsinikssiistsi

• • • • • • • • • • • • • • • • • •

Blackfoot
Stories of Old

Written, translated, and edited by
Ikkináínihki Lena Heavy Shields Russell
and *Piitáákii* Inge Genee

Illustrated by *Api'soomaahka*
William Singer III

FIRST NATIONS
UNIVERSITY
OF CANADA

SIFC

University of Regina Press

Copyright © 2014 *Ikkináínihki* Lena Heavy Shields Russell and *Piitáákii* Inge Genee

All rights reserved. No part of this work covered by the copyrights hereon may
be reproduced or used in any form or by any means—graphic, electronic, or
mechanical—without the prior written permission of the publisher. Any request
for photocopying, recording, taping or placement in information storage and
retrieval systems of any sort shall be directed in writing to Access Copyright.

Printed and bound in Canada at Friesens. The text of this book is printed on 100%
post-consumer recycled paper with earth-friendly vegetable-based inks.

COVER AND TEXT DESIGN: Duncan Campbell, University of Regina Press.

EDITOR FOR THE PRESS: Donna Grant, University of Regina Press.

The artwork in this volume was produced by *Api'soomaahka* William Singer III from the
Kaina First Nation, Alberta.

LIBRARY AND ARCHIVES CANADA CATALOGUING IN PUBLICATION
Cataloguing in Publication (CIP) data available at the Library and Archives Canada
web site: *www.collectionscanada.gc.ca* and at *www.uofrpress.ca/publications/Blackfoot-stories*

10   9   8   7   6   5   4   3   2   1

University of Regina Press, University of Regina
Regina, Saskatchewan, Canada, S4S 0A2
TEL: (306) 585-4758 FAX: (306) 585-4699
U OF R PRESS   WEB: www.uofrpress.ca

The University of Regina Press acknowledges the support of the Creative Industry
Growth and Sustainability program, made possible through funding provided to the
Saskatchewan Arts Board by the Government of Saskatchewan through the Ministry of
Parks, Culture, and Sport. We also acknowledge the financial support of the Government
of Canada through the Canada Book Fund for our publishing activities. We acknowledge
the support of the Canada Council for the Arts for our publishing program.

CONTENTS

Foreword

This is the third memoir in our First Nations Language Readers series, and I am extremely pleased that we are able to present this collection of Blackfoot texts from the Elder and linguist team of Lena Heavy Shields Russell and Inge Genee. This marks a significant expansion of our series in a number of ways.

When the series was begun through the Canadian Plains Research Center (CPRC) in 2007, its purpose was to highlight the First Nations languages of Saskatchewan and surrounding area, especially those taught at First Nations University of Canada (the former Saskatchewan Indian Federated College [SIFC]). Indeed, the first two volumes highlighted Cree and Saulteaux (Ojibwe), with texts largely from Treaty 4 and Treaty 6 territory in Saskatchewan, though some contributions were from Treaty 5 territory in Manitoba. Although the original mandates of SIFC and the CPRC were fairly constrained (to Saskatchewan and the Great Plains respectively), it was always hoped that we could grow beyond both provincial and institutional boundaries.

With the publication of this volume, we have begun this process and are proud to offer this collection of texts from

Treaty 7 territory in Alberta, as presented by my colleagues at the Kaina (Blood) Reserve and the University of Lethbridge. This has been greatly facilitated by the expansion and increased mandates of the First Nations University of Canada and of the CPRC in its new incarnation as the University of Regina Press.

The future of the First Nations Language Readers series is wide open and it is hoped we will soon be able to offer volumes in an ever-increasing number of First Nations languages from across Canada. This third memoir is an important step on the journey. I am certain that readers will enjoy this publication, the Blackfoot stories and artwork within, and the opportunity to begin or augment their learning of this beautiful language. I also invite First Nations storytellers and linguists working with these remarkable languages to take up the challenge and produce future volumes in this series.

Arok Wolvengrey
iitáómatapapittssko, 2013

Preface

When we first met in 1998, we didn't know that it would be the beginning of a longstanding friendship that would develop from a working relationship into one between friends and, indeed, family. Over the years we have learned so much from each other, about Blackfoot, about linguistics, about each other's culture, and about life. We have helped each other through high and low points, always learning from the other person's point of view, so different because of our different backgrounds. And always we would return to the study of *Niitsí'powahsini*, the Blackfoot language, our joint passion.

Over the years we created quite a large collection of stories. After a while we decided it would be a good idea to share some of them in book form. That way other people can enjoy them as well and hopefully benefit from them. We hope that fluent speakers can use them to improve their reading skills. We hope that people learning Blackfoot can use them to acquire some common words and sentence structures. And we hope that people all over the world can get an idea of what the Blackfoot language is like.

Lena Russell's Blackfoot name is *Ikkináínihki* 'Gentle Singer'; she is a fluent speaker of Blackfoot from the Kaina (Blood) reserve in southern Alberta, Canada. A certified teacher, she attended the University of Alberta and received her B.Ed. and Professional Diploma from the University of Lethbridge. She has taught all levels in regular classrooms and was one of the first teachers of the Blackfoot language; she taught in primary and secondary schools, as well as at the university and college level and in adult education centers, both on and off reserve. In addition, she is a developer of Blackfoot language curriculum and has published thirteen resource books. These are the first Blackfoot resource books that were ever published and approved by Alberta Education. Because of all her work on Blackfoot curriculum development and language teaching the University of Lethbridge awarded her an honourary doctorate in 2006. She is now retired after having been in education for almost fifty years. She is still involved in teaching the Blackfoot language and continues to be actively involved in community work, on boards and committees, as a mentor and adviser.

Lena has eight children and several grandchildren and great-grandchildren. Her father was the late Eddie Heavy Shield Sr. Her mother was the late Adelaide Fox. Both of them appear in some of the stories in this collection. Her paternal great-grandfather was *Issokoyaawo'taan* 'Heavy Shield', also called *I'ksskimmiohkinni* 'One who wears a medallion'. He was a warrior and a chief of his clan, the *Ni'taiitsskaiksi* 'Lone Fighters'.

Lena is a member of the Brave Dog society on the Blood reserve. Some of her children and grandchildren are also Brave Dog society members.

Inge Genee's Blackfoot name is *Piitáákii* 'Eagle Woman'. She is a linguist at the University of Lethbridge. She has been studying Blackfoot since 1998, and has worked with Lena from the beginning. She has published and presented on various languages, including English, Dutch, Irish, and Blackfoot.

She has two children. She was born and raised in The Netherlands and has lived with her Canadian husband and children in Canada since 1997. She received a B.A. in Dutch language and literature, and an M.A. and a Ph.D. in linguistics from the University of Amsterdam. She has lived and worked in The Netherlands, the United States, England and, since 1997, in Canada.

Acknowledgements

We are very grateful to the following people who have given us encouragement, support and assistance.

Professor Don Frantz of the University of Lethbridge took a critical look at our morpheme glosses, which resulted in improvements to the glossary. The dictionary he co-authored with Lena's daughter Norma Russell (Frantz & Russell 1995) has been a valuable resource to us, as has his *Blackfoot Grammar* (Frantz 2009). We are also grateful to him for allowing us to use an electronic version of the new edition of the dictionary.

William Singer III made the beautiful illustrations that accompany the stories.

Michaela DeBeyer assisted with the initial recording and transcription of some of the stories. Anfernee Zhou helped with the proofreading of the first two stories and the glossary. Titilola Babalola and Madoka Mizumoto proofread the whole glossary for us.

Arok Wolvengrey of the First Nations University of Canada has been encouraging and helpful throughout the publishing process.

We are grateful to the University of Lethbridge for financial assistance for this project in the form of a Community Research Excellence Development Opportunities Grant and a University of Lethbridge Research Dissemination Grant.

And last, but not least, we are both grateful to our families for their continued support and assistance. We could not have finished this book without them.

Introduction

This is the third in a series of readers in the First Nations languages of the Canadian prairie provinces meant for language learners and language users. The first volume, *Funny Little Stories* (2007), contained nine stories in the Cree language. The second volume, *Nēnapohš Legends* (2011) contained seven stories in Saulteaux (Ojibwe). This third volume adds eight stories in Blackfoot.

The Blackfoot language is spoken in Alberta, Canada, and Montana, USA, in four communities: *Kaina* (Blood), *Piikani* (Peigan) or *Aapatohsipikani* (North Peigan), *Siksika* (Blackfoot), and *Aamsskaapipikani* (Southern Piikani, Blackfeet). Blackfoot is an Algonquian language, related to such neighbouring languages as Cree, Cheyenne, and Arapaho. It is difficult to estimate how many speakers there are, but it is clear that the most fluent speakers tend to be elders, that the number of fluent speakers is diminishing, and that very few young people are learning the language in the home (Frantz n.d.; Frantz 2009: viii; Frantz & Russell 1995: xii; Genee & Russell 2006). So the Blackfoot language is quite endangered. The language is also undergoing changes, so that the modern or New Blackfoot spoken by the younger generations is quite different from the traditional Old Blackfoot spoken by the older generation (Chatsis et al. 2013).

The stories presented here were all told or written by Lena Russell between 2008 and 2012. Some were first audio-recorded and then transcribed and translated. Others were written directly for this collection.

This volume ends with a Blackfoot-to-English glossary which contains all the lexical items found in the texts. The glossary follows as closely as possible the presentation in Frantz & Russell (1995), so that the reader can look up items there as well. Some notes on the presentation are given preceding the glossary.

Blackfoot spelling

In contrast with what is customary for some other Algonquian languages, such as Cree and Saulteaux (Ojibwe) as presented in the first two volumes in this series, Blackfoot is not usually written in syllabics. Some attempts have been made to adapt the syllabic writing system for Blackfoot, and it is certainly possible to represent Blackfoot words in syllabics, but such a writing system has not been generally adopted and is not in common use. We have chosen, therefore, to give our stories only in Roman alphabet.

There is not full agreement about the best writing system for Blackfoot, but most people use a version of the spelling system devised by Donald Frantz as presented in his *Blackfoot Grammar* (Frantz 2009) and in the dictionary he co-authored with Norma Russell (Frantz & Russell 1995). This spelling system is based on the conventions of the International Phonetic Alphabet (IPA 1999), and should thus be fairly transparent for native speakers of Blackfoot, as well as for linguists. It is, however, less easy to use for those whose first language is English or for Blackfoot speakers who have first learned to read and write in English and are learning to read and write the Blackfoot language later in life. Lena Russell has always used the Frantz spelling system in her own publications (see, for example, Russell 1996–1998 and Russell 2001–2003), and we do the same here.

The basic principles of the Blackfoot spelling system are described in Frantz 2009 (Chapter 1 and Appendices C and D) and in Frantz & Russell 1995 (Appendix). For those not familiar with these sources we explain the most important points here. Of course, nothing can fully replace hearing a fluent speaker pronounce the words, but we hope this explanation may give the reader an idea of approximately how the words sound when spoken.

The following letters are used in the Blackfoot spelling system, given in the order in which they are alphabetized: a, h, i, k, m, n, o, p, s, t, w, y, '. We will discuss first the consonants and then the vowels. Where appropriate we include the IPA symbol that best corresponds to the sound or sounds represented by each letter. Such symbols are indicated in square brackets: [ ]. Not all details of the sound system of Blackfoot are fully described as yet.

The Blackfoot alphabet uses eight consonant symbols: p, t, k, s, m, n, h, and '. The first six of these are pronounced very much like in English. The main difference is that the voiceless stops p, t and k are never aspirated as in English, and therefore some Blackfoot words that contain these may sound to English speakers like they contain the voiced stops b, d, and g instead.

The last two letters in the list represent sounds that do not occur in English. The letter h represents a velar fricative much like the sound usually written as ch in German or in the Scottish word *loch* for 'lake'. Its exact pronunciation depends on the preceding vowel. After a back vowel such as a or **o**, it is pronounced with the tongue more in the back of the mouth (voiceless uvular fricative $[\chi]$). After a front vowel such as **i**, it is pronounced with the tongue more to the front (voiceless palatal fricative $[\varsigma]$). The letter **h** also occurs at the beginning of a few words, such as in the expression *hánnia* 'really!' Here it sounds very much like an English **h**.

The symbol ' represents a glottal stop (IPA symbol $[\mathsf{?}]$). This sound occurs in English in the middle of expressions such as *uh-oh!* It also may occur between two words when the first one ends with a vowel and the second one begins with the same vowel, such as *she eats*. In some British accents, it may appear in place of the **tt** in words such as *butter*. It is made by briefly closing the vocal folds and releasing them again, creating a short interruption of the airflow. In Blackfoot this sound is distinctive and therefore needs to be represented in the spelling system. The glottal stop symbol is alphabetized after all other letters.

The letters **w** and **y** represent so-called glides or semi-vowels. They sound very much like their English counterparts and present no problems in the pronunciation.

The Blackfoot alphabet uses three vowel symbols: **a**, **i**, and **o**. Their exact pronunciation can vary depending on the surrounding sounds in the rest of the word and is never exactly the same as in English, so the following are approximations. There are also some dialect differences, with people from different Blackfoot-speaking communities pronouncing some vowels slightly differently than others.

The letter **a** usually sounds like in *father* or *but* ($[\alpha]$, $[\Lambda]$). The letter **i** usually sounds like in *beat* or *bit* ($[i]$, $[\mathsf{I}]$). The letter **o** usually sounds like in *so, horse* or *book* ($[o]$, $[\mathsf{o}]$, $[\mathsf{o}]$).

When occurring at the end of a word, vowels in Blackfoot are often voiceless (whispered) and may be hard to hear, especially in words that end in *-wa*.

In addition to these three vowel letters by themselves, combinations of two vowels are used to represent additional vowel sounds. The symbol **ai** usually sounds like in *bed* or *bade* ([ɛ], [e], [eɪ]). When it sounds like in *bade* we write it as **aii**. The symbol **ao** usually sounds like in *horse* or *loud* ([ɔ], [aʊ]). The symbol **oi** usually sounds like in *boy* (IPA [ɔɪ]). The symbol **oii** sounds like in *we* (IPA [wi]).

Most Blackfoot letters occur in single and double form. This is because many Blackfoot sounds can be either long (geminate) or short. When they are long, we write them double. All consonants except for **h** and ' can be long, and vowels can be long as well.

Stress or pitch accent is not always marked in Blackfoot texts. For fluent speakers of the language, it is not necessary to mark stress, because they already know where it belongs. In this collection, we attempt to represent it as carefully as possible by marking it with an acute accent over the vowel or vowels which bear the accent on the original recordings. We do this because knowing where the stress is makes it much easier to pronounce the word correctly, so we hope this will help those who are trying to read unfamiliar words out loud. In the glossary we include the lexical accent over each entry as given in Frantz & Russell (1995). Sometimes this does not exactly match what we have in our recordings.

Blackfoot nouns

Nouns in Blackfoot are classified as animate or inanimate. As can be expected, most nouns referring to living beings such as people and animals are animate. However, grammatical gender and natural gender do not always overlap; in particular, many nouns referring to inanimate objects and concepts are also animate. In such cases, the grammatical gender is used to classify the noun, not the natural gender.

Animate nouns are marked *nan* in the glossary, and inanimate nouns are marked *nin*.

Nouns in Blackfoot have different suffixes depending on whether they are animate or inanimate and singular or plural. Animate singular nouns end in *–(w)a* (PROXIMATE) or *–(y)i* (OBVIATIVE), and animate plural nouns end in *–iksi*. Inanimate singular nouns end in *–(y)i*, and inanimate plural nouns end in *–istsi*. Where the noun reference is non-specific, a non-specific affix *–i* occurs on both animate and inanimate nouns (Frantz 2009: Chapter 2). The following examples are taken from our texts:

	ANIMATE	INANIMATE
Singular	*naaáhs-**a*** 'my grandmother'	*moohssokó-**yi*** 'road'
Plural	*maaáhs-**iksi*** 'his grandparents'	*maatáák-**istsi*** 'potatoes'
Obviative	*áwakaasii-**yi*** 'a deer'	n/a
Non-specific	*áwakaas-**i*** '(some) deer'	*í'ksisako-**i*** '(some) meat'

When looking up a noun in the glossary, the first letter of the word is not always the first letter of the glossary item. This is because nouns in Blackfoot may have various kinds of grammatical prefixes or other elements in front of the stem.

For instance, possessed nouns are marked with a possessive prefix. These have the following shapes (plural possessors also have suffixes, but we ignore these here, see Frantz 2009: Chapter 14):

PERSON	PREFIX	TRANSLATION
1st person	**n-** / **nit-**	'my, our'
2nd person	**k-** / **kit-**	'your' (sg and pl)
3rd person	**w-** / **o-** / **ot-** / **m-**	'his, her, their'

Some examples from our texts include: *n-iksíssta* '**my** mother'; *o-píkkiaakio'ksisakoomistsi* '**her** hamburger'; *kit-sínihka'simi* '**your** name'; *m-aaáhsiksi* '**his** grandparents'. Person prefixes do not occur in the glossary and must be stripped off before you look the item up. Most words referring to kinship terms ('mother', 'father', 'sister', 'grandparents') and body parts ('arm', 'nose') always must have a possessor and will never occur without such a prefix. Such obligatorily possessed nouns are called relational nouns and are indicated as *nar* (animate relational noun) or *nir* (inanimate relational noun).

In addition to possessive prefixes, other modifying elements may also precede the noun. In English, these would usually be separate words, such as adjectives, but in Blackfoot these may be part of the noun. For instance, the word *kipitáákiiwa* means 'old lady'. You would find this word under **kipita**, which means 'old, elderly, aged' and under **aakíí**, which means 'lady, woman'. Modifying elements like **kipita** are called adjuncts (*adt*) by Frantz and are marked as such in the glossary.

Blackfoot verbs

Blackfoot verb stems, like verbs in other Algonquian languages, have different forms depending on transitivity and animacy, that is, whether they are transitive or intransitive and whether their subject or object is animate or inanimate (Frantz 2009: Chapter 7). For instance, in the glossary you find two verbs that mean 'eat': **oowatoo** and **ooyi**. The first one is called 'transitive inanimate' (*vti*); it is the form used with an inanimate object. The second one is called 'animate intransitive' (*vai*); it is the form used when there is an animate subject and no object. Another example is the verb meaning 'know'. For this verb you find two forms: **ssksini** 'know something', used with an inanimate object (*vti*) and **ssksino** 'know someone', used with an animate object ('transitive animate'; *vta*). The last verb classification you will find is 'inanimate intransitive' (*vii*) for verbs with an inanimate subject and no object. Some more examples are given in the table below.

VERB CLASS	ABBR.	EXAMPLE	TRANSLATION
Animate intransitive (animate subject)	*vai*	**opii** **o'too** **yo'kaa**	'sit, stay' 'arrive' 'sleep'
Inanimate intransitive (inanimate subject)	*vii*	**iiyiko** **ko'kó** **soka'pii**	'be hard' 'be night' 'be good'
Transitive animate (animate object)	*vta*	**ssamm** **ssksinima'tsi** **ikimm**	'look at' 'teach' 'be kind to'
Transitive inanimate (inanimate object)	*vti*	**ipohtoo** **o'tsi** **omooni**	'bring' 'take' 'roll up'

When looking up a verb in the glossary, you will almost never find it under the first letter of the whole verb form. This is because verbs, even more than nouns, may be preceded by prefixes and other elements.

For instance, verbs may have prefixes marking their subject or object. The most commonly occurring ones have the following shapes, which are almost identical to the possessor prefixes on nouns (plural forms also have suffixes, but we ignore these here, see Frantz 2009: Chapter 4):

PERSON	PREFIX	TRANSLATION
1st person	n- / nit-	'I, me, we, us'
2nd person	k- / kit-	'you' (sg and pl)
3rd person	ot- / m-	'he, she, it, him, her'

Some examples from our texts include: *nit-sííkohtak-ayaapiaawa* 'I saw (very) many of them'; *nit-sítanikka* 'he then told **me**'; *nit-sítssksinima'tsookinnaana* 'he then taught **us**'; *nit-sítahkapohtó'pinnaaniaawa* '**we** took them home'; *kit-áínihkatsimatohpinnaana* 'we call on **you** for help'; *ot-síístawakka* 'they raised **him**'; *ot-áíí'hkssoysayi* 'when **it** dried'; *m-aahkáísskssa'pao'takssi* 'that **he** was always working'. These prefixes have to be stripped off the verb before looking it up in the glossary.

Verbs also have prefixes which indicate tense and aspect, such as future, durative or perfect. For instance, when looking up the verb form *nitáákohtsi'poyi* 'I will talk about' you first strip off the person prefix *nit-* 'I', and then you strip off the future prefix *áak-* 'will'; the rest of the verb now contains the adjunct **oht** 'about' and the verb stem **i'poyi** 'talk', which can both be found in the glossary. Tense and aspect prefixes are not included in the glossary.

In addition to person prefixes, other modifying elements may also precede the verb. In English, these would be separate words, such as auxiliaries, prepositions, adjectives or adverbs, but in Blackfoot these may be part of the verb. These elements are included separately in the glossary. A specific verb form may therefore occur in multiple places in the glossary. For instance, the verb form *ááhkssawa'tsto'si* means 'may we not lose it'. You would find this word in three places in the glossary: under **ááhk**, which means 'may'; under **saw**, which means 'not'; and finally also under **(w)a'tstoo**, which means 'lose'. The first two elements are classified as adjuncts (*adt*) and the last one is the real verb stem (*vti*).

References

Chatsis, Annabelle, Mizuki Miyashita & Debora Cole. 2013. A documentary ethnography of a Blackfoot language course: Patterns of Variationism and Standard in the organization of diversity. In *The Persistence of Language: Constructing and confronting the past and present in the voices of Jane H. Hill*. Shannon T. Bischoff, Deborah Cole, Amy V. Fountain & Mizuki Miyashita (eds.). Amsterdam and Philadelphia: John Benjamins, 257–290.

Frantz, Donald G. 2009 (second edition). *Blackfoot Grammar*. Toronto: University of Toronto Press.

Frantz, Donald G. n.d. Professional webpage at http://people.uleth.ca/~frantz/blkft.html.

Frantz, Donald G. & Norma Jean Russell. 1995 (second edition). *Blackfoot Dictionary of Stems, Roots, and Affixes*. Toronto: University of Toronto Press.

IPA. 1999. *Handbook of the International Phonetic Association. A Guide to the Use of the International Phonetic Alphabet*. Cambridge: Cambridge University Press.

Russell, Lena. 1996–1998. *Blackfoot 7, 8, 9 = Niitsi'powahsini*. Edmonton, Alberta: Duval House Publishing.

Russell, Lena. 2001–2003. *Blackfoot 10, 20, 30 = Niitsi'powahsini*. Edmonton, Alberta: Duval House Publishing / Standoff, Alberta: Kainaiwa Board of Education.

Russell, Lena Heavy Shields & Inge Genee. 2006. The Blackfoot language: Current position and future prospects. Plenary lecture, 38th Algonquian Conference, University of British Columbia, Vancouver, 27–29 October.

Ákaitsinikssiistsi

Blackfoot
Stories of Old

1.

Omohtó'totama'piihpi aahkssawá'tsto'si Niitsí'powahsini

Why the Blackfoot language is important to preserve

Our first text is not so much a story as a small essay on the importance of the Blackfoot language. It serves as an introduction to the collection.

1.   Omohtó'totama'piihpi
aahkssawá'tsto'si Niitsí'powahsini

Niitsí'powahsini niitá'po'totamá'piiwa
ááhkssawá'tsto'si.

Iihpipó'tootspa aahkáíítsi'poyio'si.

Isskóóhtsika aohkanáíítsi'poyio'pa.

Annííka náápiitapiiksi otáóótoohsaawa
iitomátapaii'stamáttstohkatoomiaawa
Naapí'powahsini.

Ki ánnohka maatsikakáttakaitapiiwa áíítsi'poyiiksi.

Pookáíksi máátattohpaistawatawa
maahkáíítsi'poyssaawa.

Akaiita'pomatapa'tsto'pa kitsíítsi'powahsinnooni.

Ánnohka ááhkoniyika'kimato'pa ááhkssawa'tsto'si.
Ááhkstammohtáíyissitapiiyio'pa!

1. Why the Blackfoot language is important to preserve

The Blackfoot language is so important that we do not lose it.

We were given in Creation to speak our language.

In the past we all spoke Blackfoot.

Then, when the non-native people came, they began to teach the English language.

And now there are not many people who speak Blackfoot anymore.

The children are no longer raised to speak Blackfoot.

We've really started to lose our Blackfoot language.

Let's try our best now not to lose it. Let's just use it!

2.

Aatsímoi'hkaani

Prayer

When we do our work on the Blackfoot language we usually begin with a prayer to the Source of Life, the Creator. We decided it would be good to do the same here.

2. Aatsímoi'hkaani

Áyo Iihtsipáítapiiyio'pi, isspómmookinnaana ánnohka ksiistsikóyihka.

Kímmokinnaana kitáínihkatsimatohpínnaana.

Kitsínihka'simi iikátowa'piiwa.

Naahkáísskssawaatoyi'tsiihpinnaana kitsínihka'simi.

Isspómmoosi nímohpapiyihpinnaaniksi.

Noohkáókamo'tsipo'tsit nímohtawaawahkaahpinnaani.

Nááhkssawoohkohtaiyissíniootspinnaana maká'piiyi.

Nááhkaikamotaahpinnaana.

Ááhkssawaohkoiikiiyi nookónnaanistsi.

Nááhkoohkaihtawa'psspinnaana.

Awáátoyistotsit nitááksowato'pinnaanistsi.

Nááhkaii'taamaissko'toohpinnaana
a'páómaahkannaaniki.

Isspómmoosa kanáítapiiwa.

Pikímmokinnaana ánnika soká'piiyika
nitáístotsipinnaani.

Nááhkssoksistawatsimaahpinnaana.

Nááhkssamipaitapiiyihpinnaana.

2. Prayer

We plead to you, Source of Life, help us this day.

Be kind to us, we call on you.

Your Name is very holy.

May we always keep Your Name holy.

Help our relatives.

Keep straight the path we walk.

May we not be hit by wrong.

May we be protected.

May nothing bad touch our homes.

May we have good fortune.

Bless the food we eat.

May we come back safe when we travel.

Help everyone.

Be kind to us for the good that we do.

May we raise our children well.

May we live a long life.

3.

Nínna Akáóhkitopiiwa #1

My father, Rides-Many-Horses #1

This is the first of two stories about
Lena's father, Rides-Many-Horses.

3.   Nínna Akáóhkitopiiwa #1

Óóki ánnohka anistá'piiwa *August, 2008.*
Nitáákohtsi'poyi nínna Akáóhkitopiiwa.

Ónni ánistayini Piáíáíkkspitowayi. Oksísstsi ánistayini Sáóáómitsikkanaayi. Otohkíímaana Issitáákii.
Óko'siksi iikákaitapiiyi. Niistówa Ikkináínihki
nitsítohkanaomahksiimayaawa.

Nínna iikááhsitapiiwa. Ikáíkimmiiwa matápiiksi.
I'tsinííkimmiiwa. Máttaiskaii'kimmiiwa óóta'siksi.
Áísskssa'pao'takiwa. Iihtáíyika'po'takiwa
nááhkitaohkooyssinnaani
nááhkitaohkoiipstópissinnaani. Iitsitápiiyiwa
otsítssawomaitaihtsiihpi paapó'sini.

Nitsiikákaissksini'pa opáítapiiysini. Iiksíyikowayi.
Áótoiikskimaawa áwakaasi nááhkitohkooysinnaani
í'ksisakoi. Áóhkitopiiwa. Iitawááwa'koyiiwa amíí
áwakaasiiyi. Iitáíkskimatsiiwayi. Iitáíyinniiwayi.
Iitáínnootatsiiwayi. Naaáhsa áíkaitaiyoohkimaawa
aahkiáápoohtsi. Nínna áóó'to'si naaáhsa
ááksikaakaotataawa. Iitáómatapiitsittsimaawa.

Iitáísi'tsiimaistsi. Nitsítaohkooyihpinnaana
í'ksisakoi. Naaáhsa nitáítakaohkayiimskookinnaana.

Nínna stsipokááwa 1910. Iitsí'niwa 1971. Nínna ki
niksíssta niisííkopotoiitapiiyi óko'sowaawaiksi.

3. My father, Rides-Many-Horses #1

Well, now it is August, 2008. I will talk
about my father, Rides-Many-Horses.

His father was called Perfect-Aim-In-The-Head.
His mother was called Shining-Here-And-There. His
wife was Wrapped-Like-A-Baby-Woman. He had many
children. Me, Gentle Singer, I am the oldest of them all.

My father was a very kind person. He cared
for people. He was kind to everyone (and everything).
He was even kind to his horses. He always worked. He
worked hard, so that we could eat, so that we could have a
place to live in. He lived when there was not any electricity.

I knew a lot about his life. It was very hard.
He went to hunt deer so that we could have some
meat to eat. He rode a horse. He then chased a deer.
He hunted it. He skinned it. He butchered it. My
grandmother would be waiting at home. When my
father came home, my grandmother would already be
building a fire. She would start to cut up the meat.

She would smoke it. We then had some meat
to eat. So then my grandmother would have a lot of
dry meat for us.

My father was born in 1910. He died in 1971.
My father and my mother had fourteen children.

4.

Nínna Akáóhkitopiiwa #2

My father, Rides-Many-Horses #2

This is the second story about Lena's father, Rides-Many-Horses.

4. Nínna Akáóhkitopiiwa #2

Nínna nímohtaii'poyi. Ikákawoyi otsíístotsi'pistsi.

Áísskssa'pao'takiwa. Iksí'nakstssimma
otáó'matapa'pao'takssi. Íksskonata'pssiwa.
Nanístssksinoawa maahkáísskssa'pao'takssi.
Nitáísskssaohkooyi'kookinnaana. Annííka
isskóóhtsika niitá'piyikowa.

Nítssksinoawa otsskáíí'sopoya'pssi.
Nitsítsiikanoannaana. Nitsítssksinima'tsookinnaana
nááhkaiksikki'tsissinnaani nitstákssinnaanistsi.
Oostóyi i'tsinííksikki'tsima.

Nínna otsiikáíksimatsimmoka matápiiksi.
Áákitsitstsi'pa i'tóííyi ááksiisoyiiwaiksi.
Nistápssiwa áísokitsinikiwa. Otó'toksisawáaakkiksi
áítsito'taohkanopiiyi a'yáítsinikisi.

Iistotsímma ákaitapiiyi otáístotsi'pi. Áákitsitapoowa
niksísstsi oksísstsi, áísstoyisattsiiyaawa. Si'kááni
áákitssoksístakio'pa.
Máátaakaissammotsiiyíwaiksaawa.
Máátaisitsipssattsiiyíwaiksaawa.

Otsíístawakka maaáhsiksi. Iksíni'pokaawa.
Otssáákiaii'nakstssi'si itayaksí'niyaiksi.
Áísookawaaniiwa, "nitsítsimmaksi'ni."
Iitotóíssksinima'tsaawa. Iihtssáksiwa
nióókskaisskskoi'pi.

Ánnimai nitááksikao'hkitsinikatawa.

4. My father, Rides-Many-Horses #2

I am talking about my father. There were many things that he went through.

He always worked. He was very young when he started to work. He was a very dependable worker. I knew him to be always working. He always worked to get food for us. Back then, in the past, the times were very hard.

I knew him to be very organized. We take after him that way. He taught us how to take care of our things. Him, he took good care of everything.

My father was met with pleasure by people. When someone came he would feed them. He was a good story-teller. Those who came to visit him would surround him when he told a story.

He lived the life of olden people and their ways (what they did). When he went to my mother's mother's (place), they avoided each other. A blanket would be hung up. They would not be seeing each other. They would not talk to each other.

He was raised by his grandparents. He was very pampered. When he was still young they both died. He used to say: "It was then I became an orphan." He then went to school. He left school in grade three.

That's where I will stop talking about him.

5.

Amíí ohkíni ki amááya náíípisstsiitapiima

A finger bone and a rag doll

This is a true story of something that happened to Lena when she was a child.

5. Amíí ohkíni ki amááya náíípisstsiitapiima

Nitsítsi'nakstssí'pi nimáttsitsitapoohpinnaana
annííhkai i'nióóyisa. Ótapi'sina
máátaitapoowaiksaawa. Niistónnaana
nitsiiksí'nakstssi'pinnaana
nimáttsitsitapoohpinnaana. Nitsítsitsipiihpinnaana.
Nitsítsito'tsiihpinnaana amííyai ohkína ki amááyai
náíípisstsiitapiima. Nitsítahkapohtó'pinnaaniaawa.

Otáíí'samiko'kohsi nitsítoohtowannaana amóóhka
itá'paisttokoowa spóóhtsi amíyi nookónnaani. Niksíssta
maatohkoíí'si'takiwa iitána'kima amíí
sipiáána'kima'tsisi. Nitsítohpokoomawa.
Nitsitssáó'takoohpinnaana. Máátsitstsi'pa
nitsítsaapihpinnaani. Annííka máátomaitáíhtsiiwa
paapó'sini.

Annííyi apinákoyi nínna nitsítssopowahtsi'sakka
nitsíto'tsiihpi amíyi ohkíni ki amííyi atapíími.
Nitá'nistahsi nitsítanikka
a'páíyaakssksipohtootaawa.
Nitáíí'ssksipohto'pinnaaniaawa.

Nímohtsiinapistotootspinnaaniaawa.

5. A finger bone and a rag doll

When I was young, one time we went to a house of the dead. People did not go there. Us, we were very young when we went there. We went in there. We took a bone and a rag doll. We took them home.

When it was late at night we heard someone walking about noisily up there on the roof of our house. My mother, who was not afraid of anything, lit a lantern. I went with her. We went around (the house) outside. There was nothing that we saw. At that time there was no electricity yet.

When it was the next day my dad asked me where I had picked up the bone and the doll. When I answered him he told me to return them. We took them back.

We were haunted by them.

6.

Ksíssta'pssiwa

A spirit

As in the previous story, the events related here actually happened to Lena when she was young.

6. Ksíssta'pssiwa

Amóóhka stsííwa isskóóhtsika. Niistówa ki amáá
nisíssa nitsiikáísskaii'kimmokinnaana amáá
kipitáákiiwa. Nitáísskssaitapoohpinnaana.
Nitáíí'tsiniaii'stamattsookinnaana.
Nitáísskssaohpoka'paissiimannaana.
Nimáttayakiitohkokkinnaana ponokáómitai.

Stapoíínnaaniki nimáttaooyiistotookinnaana.
Nitsiikáíyaahsowato'pinnaani oniitá'pihkiitaanistsi,
otsímmistsiihkiitaanistsi maatáákistsi, ki
opíkkiaakio'ksisakoomistsi.
Nitsiiksíkimmokinnaana.

Ámohka ko'kówa nimáttsitsitotoyio'kaahpinnaana
ookóówaayi. Iikáyaksiksisstsikowa.
Nitsíítamssokanikkinnaana: "Ásaakaistooka.
Ísstsiiwoka ámohka awaasáíí'niwahka."

Máátsikaksisstsa'piiwa. Ánnihkao'ka
otsítssawomawaakaitapísskohpi Tátsikiitapiiwa.
Niníítomiaiyoohtowannaana amóóhka
ááwaasaii'niwahka. Piwóóhtsi amíí moohssokóyi
iihtssápawaasaii'niwa. Áwaasaniwa. Aakííwa.
Amáá kipitáákiiwa nitsítanikkinnaana ksíssta'pssiwa.

Annííyi apinákoyi nitsíítamssokohtsímaahpinnaana
annááhkayi aakíiwa okáíí'nssi.

6. A spirit

This happened in the past. Myself and my younger brother were loved very much by an old lady. We always went there. She explained everything to us. We were always with her. She also gave us each a horse.

When we went there, she cooked for us. We liked to eat her bannock, her fried potatoes, and her hamburgers. She loved us very much.

This certain night we went to sleep at her house. It was moonlight. All of a sudden she then told us: "Come over here for a moment. Listen to someone who is crying."

There was not a sound. That was the time when there were not very many places in Standoff. We heard someone distinctly who was crying. Far away on the road she was crying. She was mourning. It was a lady. Our old lady friend told us it is a spirit (who is crying).

The next day we heard there was a lady who died.

7.

Isstoyíísi

Cold weather

This is another story from Lena's childhood years. It describes how people kept themselves warm in winter and how they prepared for the cold weather well in advance. The moral of this story is: *áísopowatsistotoohsiyaawa*: 'They prepared'.

7. Isstoyíísi

Isskóóhtsika, áíkkamssooksstónnatsstoyiwa. Annííka máátomaitáíhtsiiwa paapó'sini. Matápiiksi áííta'pototaayaawa míístsi ki ááwaakissiyaawa.

Nínna kii niksíssta áísopowatsistotoohsiyaawa sawomáísstoyiisi. Áóhkohtaayaawa. Áíkahksiststakiyaawa. Nínna aista'toksííma miistsíístsi okahksíststakssoowaawaistsi. Máttaohpommaawa sikóóhkotoki.

Isstoyíísi nookónnaani áípanniksistoyiiwa.

7. Cold weather

In the past, once in a while it would suddenly get very cold. Back then there was no electricity. The people burned wood and hauled water.

My father and my mother would get ready before the cold weather came. They would gather firewood. They sawed wood. My father split the wood that they had sawed. He also bought coal.

In the winter our house was warm all night.

8.

Ómahksisttsííksiinaiksi

Rattlesnakes

This last story is
about rattlesnakes.

8. Ómahksisttsííksiinaiksi

Nitáákohtsitsiniki ómahksisttsííksiinaiksi.

Nitsííkohtakayaapiaawa. Nínna ííkohtakáíí'nikkiwaiksi
amíí Pináápoohtsi ki amíí Piksííksiinaikawahkoyi.
Ámohka iitsí'nitsiiwa anníiiskai
omahkáómahkimiini. Iitsí'yinniiwayi. Ki
iitsítohkitssaipsstaiwayi amííyai
apáksisttohksiksiiwa. Otáíí'hkssoysayi
iitomóóniiwayi. Áíyaakohkotsiiwayi anníiiskai
náápiikoanini. Iihkitópiiwa otáíí'tapomaahkaani
amíí náápiikoani ookóówaayi.
Máátohkoonoyiiwaatsi amíí otokísi.

Amáá ómahksisttsiiksiinaawa aii'yíínapi'takisi
áíí'tstsi'pa i'sskáána'pi iitáísattsikotoyiiwa.
ómahksisttsííksiinaiksi iiksí'sskaana'pssiyi.

Ki ánnai naanístohtsitsiniki ómahksisttsííksiinaiksi.

8. Rattlesnakes

I'm going to tell a story about rattlesnakes.

I saw many of them. My father killed several of them at the North End and at Snake Coulee. At one time he killed a huge one. He skinned it. And he stretched it on a board to dry. When it dried, he rolled it up. He was going to give it to a white man. He was on horseback when he went to the white man's house. He couldn't find the skin.

When a rattlesnake senses danger, his rattles move and make a sound. Rattlesnakes are very dangerous.

That's my story about rattlesnakes.

Blackfoot-English Glossary

Presentation

This glossary contains all the lexical items occurring in our texts. As much as possible, all headword entries in this glossary are given as in Donald G. Frantz and Norma Jean Russell's *Blackfoot Dictionary of Stems, Roots and Affixes* (University of Toronto Press, 2nd edition, 1995; abbreviated F&R). The reader is referred to F&R for more information and examples of each entry. Some glossary entries do not occur as headword entries in F&R, but are included under a related entry as a "related stem" (see F&R xvi); these are not specially indicated in our glossary, since they are usually easy to find amongst similar forms.

Grammatical elements, such as person affixes, inversion, clitic pronouns, number (singular/plural), gender (animate/inanimate) as well as most tense/aspect markers (such as durative/imperfective, future, past) are not included in this glossary. The reader is referred to Frantz (2009) for details.

After the entry (in bold), the stem class code (in italics), and the gloss, examples from our texts are given between square brackets. Each example is marked with a number that indicates the text and the sentence within the text for easy reference (e.g., "2.6" means: 'text 2, sentence 6'). The part of the word from our texts that represents the entry is indicated in bold. The form of many entries may change under the influence of neighbouring elements in a word, so again, the indicated word part is often not completely identical to the headword entry.

Forms not occurring in F&R are marked with an asterisk (*). Some forms which do not occur in F&R (second edition) will be included in the third edition, which is currently being prepared for publication. We are grateful to Don Frantz for allowing us to use an early version of this edition. Forms which occur neither in F&R nor in the forthcoming third edition are marked with a double asterisk (**).

Spelling variation

The spelling of the words in the text is not always identical to the spelling in F&R. These are not errors, but the result of our decision to represent the texts in a spelling that is as close as possible to Lena Russell's pronunciation. In some cases it represents a slightly different preference for the representation of Blackfoot sounds. We have left the headword entries as in F&R, to make it easier for the reader to look up the items in there if they want more information and examples. As explained in the introduction, the symbol ' represents a glottal stop and is alphabetized after **y**, at the very end of the alphabet.

Stress

Pitch accent (or stress) is indicated by an acute accent on the vowel or diphthong. We have kept lexical stress where indicated in F&R in the headword entries, but in the text we have represented as best as possible which syllable in each word has the main accent in Lena Russell's speech. Again, sometimes this does not agree with what F&R have.

Stem class codes

Each entry in the glossary is first followed by an abbreviation indicating its stem class (in italics) and then by a gloss which gives its meaning in English as closely as possible.

The following stem class codes are used:

adt   adjunct (modifying elements, often called preverbs and prenouns in the study of other Algonquian languages; e.g., **aisskahs** 'always', **iik** 'very') *dem*   demonstrative (elements with meanings such as 'this', 'that', in English; e.g., **amo** 'this')

nan   animate noun (a noun of animate gender; e.g., **aakíí** 'woman')

nar   animate relational noun (an animate noun which must have a possessor, often called dependent nouns in the study of other Algonquian languages; e.g., **oko's** 'child')

nin   inanimate noun (a noun of inanimate gender; e.g., **immistsííhkiitaan** 'fry bread')

nir   inanimate relational noun (an inanimate noun which must have a possessor, often called dependent nouns in the study of other Algonquian languages; e.g., **ookóówa** 'house')

pro   pronoun

und   uninflected word (words which do not take any inflection; e.g., **ki** 'and')

vai   animate intransitive verb (a verb which takes an animate subject and no object; e.g., **á'po'taki** 'work')

vii   inanimate intransitive verb (a verb which takes an inanimate subject and no object; e.g., **soka'pii** 'be good')

vta   transitive animate verb (a verb which takes a subject and an animate object; e.g., **oksisawaaat** 'visit someone')

vti   transitive inanimate verb (a verb which takes a subject and an inanimate object; e.g., **o'tsi** 'take something')

aaáhs *nar* elder relation [**naaáhs**a 'my grandmother', 3.23, 3.24, 3.28; **maaáhs**iksi 'his grandparents', 4.22]

ááhk *adt* might, may/NONFACTIVE [**ááhk**ssawa'tsto'si 'may we not lose it', 1.1; 1.8; **aahk**áíítsi'poyio'si 'that we might speak Blackfoot', 1.2; **maahk**áíítsi'poyssaawa 'that they might speak Blackfoot', 1.6; **ááhk**oniyika'kimato'pa 'let us try hard', 1.8; **ááhk**stammohtáíyissitapiiyio'pa 'let's just use it', 1.9; **naahk**áísskssawaatoyi'tsiihpinnaana 'may we always keep it holy', 2.4; **nááhk**ssawoohkohtaiyissíniootspinnaana 'may we not be hit', 2.7; **nááhk**aikamotaahpinnaana 'may we be protected', 2.8; **ááhk**ssawaohkoiikiiyi 'may nothing bad touch them', 2.9; **nááhk**oohkaihtawa'psspinnaana 'may we have good fortune', 2.10; **nááhk**aii'taamaissko'toohpinnaana 'may we come back safe', 2.12; **nááhk**ssoksistawatsimaahpinnaana 'may we raise (our children) well', 2.15; **nááhk**ssamipaitapiiyihpinnaana 'may we live a long life', 2.16; **nááhk**itaohkooyssinnaani 'so that we might have something to eat', 3.13; **nááhk**itaohkoiipstópissinnaani 'so that we could have a place to live in', 3.13; **nááhk**itohkooysinnaani 'so that we could have something to eat', 3.17; **maahk**áísskssa'pao'takssi 'that he was always working', 4.6; **nááhk**aiksikki'tsissinnaani 'how to take care of them', 4.11]

aahs *adt* pleasing, good, nice, kind [see **yaahs**]

aakíí *nan* woman [Issitáákii 'Wrapped-Like-A-Baby-Woman' (name), 3.5; kipitáákiiwa 'old lady', 6.2; **aakíí**wa 'she/there was a lady', 6.20, 6.22]

aanist *adt* manner [**anist**á'piiwa 'it is', 3.1;
na**níst**ssksinoawa 'I knew him', 4.6; **(a)nist**ápssiwa
'he was', 4.15; na**aníst**ohtsitsiniki '(in this way) I tell a
story about', 8.13]

aapinákos *nin* tomorrow, next day [**apináko**yi 'the next
day', 5.13; 6.22]

aato* *adt* holy, sacred [see **naato**]

aatsímoyihkaan *nin* prayer, religion [**aatsimoi'hkaan**i
'prayer', 2.title]

ááyo* *und* 'we plead to you' (exclamation used in prayers)
[2.1]

áísooka* *adt* formerly [**áísooka**waaniiwa 'he used to say',
4.25]

aisskahs *adt* always [naahk**áísskssa**waatoyi'tsiihpinnaana
'may we always keep it holy', 2.4;
áísskssa'pao'takiwa 'he was always working', 3.12,
4.3; maahk**áísskss**a'pao'takssi 'that he was always
working', 4.6; nit**áísskss**aohkooyi'kookinnaana
'he always worked to get food for us', 4.7;
nitsiik**áísska**ii'kimmokinnaana 'she always
loved us very much', 6.2; nit**áísskss**aitapoohpinnaan
'we always went there', 6.3;
nit**áísskss**aohpoka'paissiimannaana
'we were always with her', 6.5][1]

áíssksinimá'tsaa *nan* student [iitotó**íssksinima'tsaa**wa
'then he went to school' (lit. 'then he went to be a
student'), 4.26]

---

1   See Frantz 2009: 103–104.

aist *adt* here, toward location of speaker [ásaak**aist**ooka 'could you come over here for a moment' 6.13]

aká *adt* many [see **waaka**]

ákaitapii *nan* person of the past [**ákaitapii**yi 'olden people', 4.17]

akáítapissko *nin* town, place of many people [otsítssawomawa**akaitapíssko**hp 'there were not yet many places', 6.16]

am *dem* this, close to speaker [**am**íí, 3.19, 5.8, 6.18, 8.3 (2x), 8.9, 8.10; **am**ííyai, 5.5; **am**ááya, 5.5; **am**íyi, 5.7, 5.13; **am**áá, 6.2 (2x), 6.21, 8.11]

amo *dem* this, close to speaker but not addressee [**am**óóhka, 5.7, 6.1, 6.17; **ámo**hka, 6.10, 6.14, 8.4]

aná'kimaa'tsis *nin* lamp [sipiá**ána'kima'tsis**i 'a night lantern', 5.8]

ann *dem* that, close to addressee but not speaker [**ann**ííka 'back then, at that time', 1.4, 4.8, 5.12, 7.2; **ánn**ika, 2.14; **ánn**imai 'that's where', 4.28; **ann**ííyi 'it was then', 5.13, 6.22; **ánn**ihkao'ka 'that was when', 6.16; **ann**ááhkayi 'that there was', 6.22; **ann**íiiskai 'that one', 8.4, 8.8; ki-**ánn**ai 'and that is', 8.13]

anniika** *und* then [see **ann**]

anno *dem* this, close to speaker and addressee [**ánno**hka 'now', 1.5, 1.7, 3.1; 'this', 2.1]

annohk *und* now [see **anno**]

apaksísttohksiksis *nin* board, lumber [**apáksisttohksiksii**wa 'a board', 8.6]

assaak *adt* stop and VERB for a moment [**ásaak**aistooka 'could you come over here for a moment' 6.13]

atapíím *nan* doll [náíípisstsi**itapiim**a 'rag doll', 5.5; **atapíím**i 'doll', 5.13]

att *adt* again [see **matt**]

áwákaasii *nan* deer, antelope [**áwakaasi** 'deer', 3.17; **áwakaasii**yi 'a deer', 3.19]

á'p *adt* about, around [**a'p**áómaahkannaaniki 'when we travel about', 2.12; itá**'p**aisttokoowa 'she was walking about there noisily', 5.7; **a'p**áíyaakssksipohtootaawa 'bring them back!', 5.14; áíít**a'p**ototaayaawa 'they made fire', 7.3]

a'paissi** *vai* spend time [nitáísskssaohpok**a'paissi**imannaana 'we were always with her', 6.5]

a'pii *vii* be in a specified way [iikátow**a'pii**wa 'it is very holy', 2.3; anist**á'pii**wa 'it is', 3.1; máátsikaksissts**a'pii**wa 'there was not a sound', 6.15]

á'po'taki *vai* work [áísskss**a'pao'taki**wa 'he was always working', 3.12, 4.3; iihtáíyik**a'po'taki**wa 'he worked very hard', 3.13; otáó'matap**a'pao'tak**ssi 'when he started to work', 4.4; maahkáísskss**a'pao'tak**ssi 'that he was always working', 4.6]

a'pssi *vai* be in a specified way [(a)nist**á'pssi**wa 'he was', 4.15]

hko *vta* provide for [nitáítakaohkayiim**sko**okinnaana 'she would have a lot for dry meat for us', 3.28]

ihkiitaa *vai* cook, bake [oniitá**'pihkiitaa**nistsi 'her bannock' (lit. 'her real cooking'), 6.8; otsímmists**iihkiitaa**nistsi 'her fried goods', 6.8]

BRESCIA UNIVERSITY COLLEGE LIBRARY

ihkitaan** *nin* cooking, baking [see **ihkiitaa**][2]

ihkssoyi *vai* become dry [otáíí'**hkssoy**sayi 'when it dried', 8.7]

ihtawa'pssi *vai* be lucky [nááhkoohka**ihtawa'pss**pinnaana 'may we have good fortune', 2.10]

ihtsii* *vai* lie (down), be, exist [otsítssawomaita**ihtsii**hpi 'there was not yet', 3.14; máátomaitá**íhtsii**wa 'there was not yet', 5.12, 7.2]

iihp *adt* with/ASSOCIATIVE [see **ohp**]

iihsiss *nar* younger sibling of female [nisíssa 'my younger brother', 6.2]

iiht *adt* through, by, about/INSTRUMENT/SOURCE/ MEANS/CONTENT (see **oht**)

Iihtsipáítapiiyo'pa *nan* Creator, God, lit. 'the one through whom we live' [**Iihtsipáítapiiyio'pa** 'Source of Life', 2.1]

iik *adt* very/INTENSIFIER [maats**ik**akáttakaitapiiwa 'there are not very many people', 1.5; **iik**átowa'piiwa 'it is very holy', 2.3; **iik**ákaitapiiyi 'they were very many people', 3.6; **iik**ááhsitapiiwa 'he was a very kind person', 3.8; nits**iik**ákaissksini'pa 'I knew a lot about', 3.15; **iik**síyikowayi 'it was very hard', 3.16; **ik**ákawoyi 'they were many', 4.2; **ik**sí'nakstssimma 'he was very young', 4.4; **ík**sskonata'pssiwa 'he was very industrious (i.e. a very dependable worker)', 4.5; ots**iik**áíksimatsimmoka 'he was very much

appreciated', 4.13; **iksíni'pokaawa** 'he was very
pampered', 4.23; nits**iiksí'nakstssí'pinnaana** 'we were
very young', 5.3; nits**iikáísskaii'kimmokinnaana**
'she always loved us very much', 6.2;
nits**iikáíyaahsowato'pinnaani** 'we very much liked
to eat', 6.8; nits**iiksíkimmokinnaana** 'she loved us
very much', 6.9; **iik**áyaksiksisstsikowa 'it was (very)
clear) moonlight', 6.11; nits**ííkohtakayaapiaawa** 'I saw
(very) many of them', 8.2; **ííkohtakáíí'nikkiwaiksi** 'he
killed (very) many of them', 8.3; **iiksí'sskaana'pssiyi**
'they are very dangerous', 8.12]

iimaa *adt* yet, to the present time
[otsítssaw**oma**itaihtsiihpi 'there was not yet', 3.14;
máát**omá**ítaihtsiiwa 'there was not yet', 5.12, 7.2;
otsítssaw**oma**waakaitapísskohp 'there were not yet
many places', 6.16]

iisto *pro* PRONOMINAL BASE [n**iistó**wa 'I, me', 3.7, 6.2;
o**ostó**yi 'he, him', 4.12; n**iistó**nnaana 'we, us', 5.3]

iit *adt* there, then + PAST TENSE [see **it**]

iitsi'poyi *vai* speak Blackfoot [aahk**áíítsi'poyi**o'si
'that we might speak Blackfoot', 1.2;
aohkan**áíítsi'poyi**o'pa 'we all spoke Blackfoot', 1.3;
áíítsi'poyiiksi 'those who speak Blackfoot', 1.5;
maahk**áíítsi'poy**ssaawa 'that they might speak
Blackfoot', 1.6]

ííyik *adt* hard, strong, fervent [iiht**áíyik**a'po'takiwa 'he
worked very hard', 3.13]

iiyika'kimaatoo *vti* try hard to [ááhkon**iyika'kimato**'pa
'let us try hard', 1.8]

iiyiko *vii* be hard, difficult [iiksíyikowayi 'it was very hard', 3.16; niitá'piyikowa 'it was truly hard', 4.8]

ikahksiststaki *vai* saw (wood) [áíkahksiststakiyaawa 'they sawed wood', 7.6; okahksíststakssoowaawaistsi '(that) they had sawed', 7.7]

ikak *adt* just, only, even [maatsikakáttakaitapiiwa 'there are not very many people', 1.5; máátsikaksisstsa'piiwa 'there was not (even) a sound', 6.15]

ikamotaa *vai* survive, escape, recover [nááhkaikamotaahpinnaana 'may we be protected', 2.8]

ika' *adt* for now, presently [nitááksikao'hkitsinikatawa 'I will stop talking about him', 4.28]

ikii *vai* do to, happen to [ááhkssawaohkoiikiiyi 'may nothing bad happen to them', 2.9]

ikimm *vta* show kindness to, care for [kímmokinnaana 'be kind to us', 2.2; pikímmokinnaana 'be kind to us (for)', 2.14; ikáíkimmiiwa 'he cared for them', 3.9; i'tsinííkimmiiwa 'he was kind to everyone and everything', 3.10; máttaiskaii'kimmiiwa 'he was very kind to them', 3.11; nitsiikáísskaii'kimmokinnaana 'she always loved us very much', 6.2; nitsiiksíkimmokinnaana 'she loved us very much', 6.9]

ikkam *adt* fast, quickly [áíkkamssooksstonnatsstoyiwa 'it would suddenly get extremely cold', 7.1]

ikkana *vai* glitter, sparkle, shine [Sáóáómitsikkanaayi 'Shining-Here-And-There' (name), 3.4]

46

ikkina *adt* gentle, slow, soft [**Ikkináínihki** 'Gentle Singer' (name), 3.7]

iksikki'tsi* *vti* take care of [nááhka**iksikki'tsi**ssinnaani 'how to take care of them', 4.11; i'tsiníí**ksikki'tsi**ma 'he took good care of everything', 4.12]

iksimatsimm *vta* greet [otsiiká**íksimatsimm**oka 'he was greeted with pleasure', 4.13]

iksísst *nar* mother [**oksíssts**i 'his mother', 3.4; n**iksíssts**i 'my mother', 4.18; **oksíssts**i 'her mother', 4.18; n**iksíssta** 'my mother', 5.8, 7.4]

iksistoyi *vii* be warm [áípann**iksistoyi**iwa 'it was warm all night', 7.9]

ikskimaa *vai* hunt game [áótoi**kskimaa**wa 'he went to hunt', 3.17]

ikskimat *vta* hunt game [iitá**íkskimat**siiwayi 'then he hunted it', 3.20]

immaksi'ni *vai* be orphaned at a young age [nitsíts**immaksi'ni** 'then I became an orphan', 4.25]

immistsííhkiitaan *nin* fried goods, fry bread [otsí**mmistsiihkiitaan**istsi 'her fried goods', 6.8]

inap* *adt* sense [aii'yíí**napi**'takisi 'when it senses', 8.11]

inihka'sim* *nin* name [kitsí**nihka'sim**i 'your name', 2.3, 2.4]

inihkatsimat *vta* call on someone for help [kitá**inihkatsimat**ohpinnaana 'we call on you for help', 2.2]

inihki *vai* sing [Ikkiná**inihki** 'Gentle Singer' (name), 3.7]

inii'pokaa *vai* be spoiled, given special treatment as a
child [iks**íni'pokaa**wa 'he was very pampered', 4.23]

inn *nar* father [n**ínn**a 'my father', 3.2, 3.8, 3.24, 3.29, 3.31,
4.1, 4.13, 5.13, 7.4, 7.7, 8.3; ó**nn**i 'his father', 3.3]

innootat *vta* skin, butcher [iitá**innootat**siiwayi 'then he
butchered it', 3.22]

ipaitapiiyi *vai* live, be alive [Iihts**ipáítapiiyi**o'pi 'source
of life, Creator, God', lit. 'the one through whom we
live', 2.1; nááhkssam**ipaitapiiyi**hpinnaana 'may we
live a long life, 2.16; o**páítapiiy**sini 'his life', 3.15]

ipann *adt* overnight [á**ípann**iksistoyiiwa 'it was warm
all night', 7.9]

ipii *vai* enter [nitsíts**ipii**hpinnaana 'we went in there', 5.4]

ipii *adt* far, long distance, remote in space
[**Pi**áííkksspitowayi 'Shoots-From-Afar' (name), 3.3;
piwóóhtsi 'far away', 6.18]

ipohtoo *vti* bring [nitsítahka**pohtó**'pinnaaniaawa
'we took them home', 5.6;
a'páíyaakssks**ipohtoo**taawa 'bring them back!', 5.14;
nitáíí'ssks**ipohto**'pinnaaniaawa 'we took them back,
5.15;]

ipokaa(wa'si) *vai* be born [sts**ipokáá**wa 'he was born', 3.29]

ipo'to *vta* release, place [iihp**ipó'to**otspa 'we were placed', 1.2]

ipo'tsi *vti* let, release, keep [noohkáókamo'ts**ipo'tsi**t
'please keep it straight', 2.6]

ipsst *adt* inside [nááhkitaohkoi**ipst**opissinnaani 'so that
we could have a place to live in', 3.13]

isam *adt* long (in time) [nááhks**sam**ipaitapiiyihpinnaana 'may we live a long life', 2.16; otáíí'**sam**ikó'kohsi 'when it was late at night', 5.7]

isskoohtsik *nin* past, long ago [**isskóóhtsik**a 'in the past, long ago', 1.3, 4.8, 6.1, 7.1]

issksskoi'p* *nin* place in sequence [nióókska**issksskoi'p**i 'in grade three', 4.27]

istawat *vta* raise (a child or young animal) [máátattohpa**istawat**awa 'they are no longer raised', 1.6; otsíí**stawa**kka 'they raised him, he was raised by them', 4.22]

istawatsimaa *vai* raise children [nááhkssoks**istawatsimaa**hpinnaana 'may we raise (our children) well', 2.15]

istotsi *vti* acquire facility in, become experienced/good at, do/practice [awáátoy**istotsi**t 'bless it' (lit. 'keep it holy'), 2.11; nitá**istotsi**pinnaani 'we do/practice it', 2.14; otsíí**stotsi**'pistsi 'the things that he went through', 4.2; i**istotsí**mma 'he lived the life', 4.17; otá**istotsi**'pi 'their ways', 4.17]

isttok** *adt* noisily [itá'pa**isttok**oowa 'she was walking about there noisily', 5.7]

it *adt* then, there, at a certain time or place [i**it**omátapaii'stamáttstohkatoomiaa 'then they began to teach', 1.4; nits**í**tohkanaomahksiimayaawa 'I am the oldest of them all', 3.7; nááhk**it**aohkooyssinnaani 'so that we might have something to eat', 3.13; nááhk**it**aohkoiipstópissinnaani 'so that we could have a place to live in', 3.13; i**it**sitápiiyiwa 'he lived then',

3.14; nááhkitohkooysinnaani 'so that we could have something to eat', 3,.13, 3.17; otsítssawomaitaihtsiihpi 'there was not yet', 3.14; iitawááwa'koyiiwa 'he then chased it', 3.19; iitáíkskimatsiiwayi 'then he hunted it', 3.20; iitáíyinniiwayi 'then he skinned it', 3.21; iitáínnootatsiiwayi 'then he butchered it', 3.22; áíkaitaiyoohkimaawa 'she would be waiting', 3.23; iitáómatapiitsittsimaawa 'then she would start to cut up the meat', 3.25; iitáísi'tsiimaistsi 'then she smoked them', 3.26; nitsítaohkooyihpinnaana 'we then had (some meat) to eat', 3.27; nitáítakaohkayiimskookinnaana 'she would have a lot of dry meat for us', 3.28; iitsí'niwa 'then he died', 3.30; nitsítsiikanoannaana 'we take after him that way', 4.10; nitsítsiikanoannaana 'he then taught us', 4.11; áítsito'taohkanopiiyi 'they would then surround him there, 4.16; áákitsitapoowa 'he went there', 4.18; áákitssoksístakio'pa 'it would be hung up, 4.19; itayaksí'niyaiksi 'then they both died', 4.24; nitsítsimmaksi'ni 'then I became an orphan', 4.25; iitotóíssksinima'tsaawa 'then he went to school' (lit. 'then he went to be a student'), 4.26; nitsitsí'nakstssí'pi 'when I was young', 5.1; nimáttsitsitapoohpinnaana 'we went there', 5.1, 5.3; nitsítsipiihpinnaana 'we went in there', 5.4; nitsítsito'tsiihpinnaana 'we took it (then and there)', 5.5; nitsítahkapohtó'pinnaaniaawa 'we took them home', 5.6; itá'paisttokoowa 'she was walking about there noisily', 5.7; nitsítoohtowannaana 'then we heard it', 5.7; iitána'kima 'she then lit a lantern', 5.8; nitsítohpokoomawa 'I went with her', 5.9; nitsitssáó'takoohpinnaana 'we went around outside', 5.10; nitsítsaapihpinnaani 'we saw', 5.11; máátomaitaihtsiiwa 'there was not yet', 5.12; nitsítssopowahtsi'sakka 'he asked

me', 5.13; nitsíto'tsiihpi 'where had I taken
it', 5.13; nitsítanikka 'he then told me', 5.14;
nimáttsitsitotoyio'kaahpinnaana 'we (then) went to
sleep (there)', 6.10; otsítssawomawaakaitapísskohpi
'there were not yet many places', 6.16;
nitsítanikkinnaan 'she then told us', 6.21;
áííta'pototaayaawa 'they made fire', 7.3; iitsí'nitsiiwa
'he then killed it', 8.4; iitsí'yinniiwayi 'then he skinned
it', 8.5; iitsítohkitssaipsstaiwayi 'then he stretched it',
8.6; iitomóóniiwayi 'then he rolled it up', 8.7]

itam *adt* only [nitsíítamssokaníkkinnaana
'all of a sudden she told us', 6.12;
nitsíítamssokohtsímaahpinnaana 'we heard the
news', 6.22]

itap *adt* toward [áákitsitapoowa 'he went there', 4.18;
nimáttsitsitapoohpinnaana 'we went there', 5.1, 5.3;
máátaitapoowaiksaawa 'they did not go there', 5.2;
nitáísskssaitapoohpinnaan 'we always went there',
6.3; stapoíínnaaniki 'when we went there', 6.7;
otáíí'tapomaahkaani 'he went there by horse', 8.9]

itapii(yi) *vai* live, be a person [náápiitapiiksi 'nonnative
people', 1.4; [maatsikakáttakaitapiiwa 'there
are not very many people', 1.5; kanáítapiiwa
'everyone', 2.13; iikákaitapiiyi 'they were very many
people', 3.6; iikááhsitapiiwa 'he was a very kind
person', 3.8; iitsitápiiyiwa 'he lived then', 3.14;
niisííkopottoiitapiiyi 'they were fourteen people',
3.31]

itsínikat *vta* tell a story of [nitááksikao'hkitsinikatawa
'I will stop talking about him', 4.28]

itsiniki *vai* tell a story [a'yá**itsiniki**si 'when he told a story, 4.16; áísok**itsiniki**wa 'he was a good storyteller', 4.15; nitáákohts**itsiniki** 'I am going to tell a story about', 8.1; naanístohts**itsiniki** 'I tell a story about', 8.13]

itsstaki *vai* have, possess [nit**sták**ssinnaanistsi 'our things', 4.11]

itsstakssin* *nin* thing, possession [nit**stákssin**naanistsi 'our things', 4.11][3]

itstsii *vii* be, exist [áákits**itstsi**'pa, 'when there was', 4.14; mááts**itstsii**'pa 'there was nothing', 5.11; **stsíí**wa 'it was, happened', 6.1; áíí**'tstsi**'pa '(when) there is', 8.11]

i'ksisako *nin* meat [**í'ksisako**i '(some) meat', 3.17, 3.27]

i'nákstssi *vai* be young, small [otssáákiaii**'nakstssi**'si 'when he was still young', 4.24; nitsitsí**'nakstssí**'pi 'when I was young', 5.1; nitsiiksí**'nakstssí**'pinnaana 'we were very young', 5.3]

i'ni *vai* die [iitsí**'ni**wa 'then he died', 3.30; itayaksí**'ni**yaiksi 'then they both died', 4.24; **i'ni**óóyisa 'a house of the dead', 5.1; okáíí**'n**ssi 'she died', 6.22]

i'nit *vta* kill [ííkohtakáíí**'nik**kiwaiksi 'he killed (very) many of them', 8.3; ; iitsí**'nit**siiwa 'he then killed it', 8.4]

i'pówahsin *nin* language, talk, speech [Niitsí**'powahsin**i 'real language', i.e. 'Blackfoot language', 1.1; Naapí**'powahsin**i 'nonnative language, i.e. English

---

language', 1.4; kitsíítsi**'powahsin**nooni 'our
Blackfoot language', 1.7]

i'poyi *vai* talk, speak [nitáákohtsi**'poyi** 'I will talk about',
3.2; nímohtaii**'poyi** 'I am talking about', 4.1]

i'si'taki** *vai* fear, distrust [maatohkóíí**'si'taki**wa 'she
was not afraid of anything', 5.8]

i'sskaana'pii *vii* be dangerous [i**'sskáána'pi** 'it is
dangerous', 8.11]

i'sskaana'pssii *vai* be dangerous [iiksí**'sskaana'pssi**yi
'they are very dangerous', 8.12]

i'táám *adt* happy, pleasant, enjoyable
[nááhkaii**'taam**aissko'toohpinnaana 'may we come
back safe (lit. 'happy')', 2.12]

i'taki *vai* feel, sense [aii'yíínapi**'taki**si 'when it senses',
8.11]

i'tsi *vti* feel emotion/attitude toward
[naahkáísskssawaatoyi**'tsi**ihpinnaana 'may we
always keep it holy', 2.4]

i'tsini *adt* everything [i**'tsini**ikimmiiwa 'he was kind to
everyone and everything', 3.10; i**'tsiníí**ksikki'tsima
'he took good care of everything', 4.12;
nitáíí**'tsini**áii'stamattsookinnaana 'she explained
everything to us', 6.4]

i'yinn* *vta* skin, remove the hide from [iitá**íyinn**iiwayi
'he skinned it', 3.21; iitsí**'yinn**iiwayi 'then he skinned
it', 8.5]

kaawahkó *nin* coulee [Piksííksiinai**kawahko**yi 'Snake
Coulee', 8.3]

káyiis *nin* dry meat, jerky
[nitáítakaoh**kayii**mskookinnaana 'she would have a
lot of dry meat for us', 3.28]

ki *und* and [1.5, 3.31, 5.5, 5.13, 6.2, 6.8, 7.3, 7.4, 8.3, 8.6, 8.13]

kipita *adt* aged, elderly [**kipitá**ákiiwa 'old lady', 6.2]

kipitáaakii *nan* old woman [**kipitáákii**wa 'old lady',
6.2, 6.21]

ko'kó *vii* be night [otáíí'sami**kó'ko**hsi 'when it was late
at night', 5.7; **ko'kó**wa 'it was night', 6.10]

ksiistsikó *nin* day [**ksiistsikó**yihka 'day', 2.1]

ksíssta'pssi *nan* spirit [**ksíssta'pssi**wa 'a spirit', 6.21]

maat *adt* not/NEGATION [**maat**sikakáttakaitapiiwa
'there are not very many people', 1.5;
máátattohpaistawatawa 'they are no longer
raised', 1.6; **máát**aakaissammotsiiyiwaiksaawa
'they would not be seeing each other', 4.20;
máátaisitsipssattsiiyíwaiksaawa 'they would not talk
to each other', 4.21; **máát**aitapoowaiksaawa 'they
did not go there', 5.2; **maat**ohkóíí'si'takiwa 'she was
not afraid of anything', 5.8; **máát**sitstsii'pa 'there was
nothing', 5.11; **máát**omaitáíhtsiiwa 'there was not
yet', 5.12, 7.2; **máát**sikaksisstsa'piiwa 'there was not
a sound', 6.15; **máát**ohkoonoyiiwaatsi 'he could not
find it', 8.10]

maatáák *nin* potato [**maatáák**istsi 'potatoes', 6.8]

maka'pii *vii* be bad [**maká'pii**yi 'bad (thing)', 2.7]

matápi *nan* person [**matápi**iksi 'people', 3.9, 4.13, 7.3]

(m)att *adt* again, additionally, even, also
[maatsikak**átt**akaitapiiwa 'there are not very
many people', 1.5; máá**tatt**ohpaistawatawa 'they
are no longer raised', 1.6; **mátt**aiskaii'kimmiiwa
'he was (even) very kind to them', 3.11;
ni**mátt**sitsitapoohpinnaana 'we went there', 5.1, 5.3;
ni**mátt**ayakiitohkokkinnaana 'she also gave to each of
us', 6.6; ni**mátt**aooyiistotookinnaana 'she also cooked
for us', 6.7; ni**mátt**sitsitotoyio'kaahpinnaana 'we went
to sleep', 6.10; **matt**aohpómmaawa 'he also bought', 7.8]

miistsís *nin* branch, stick [**míístsi** 'wood', 7.3;
miistsíístsi 'wood, branches', 7.7]

mohsokó *nin* road [**moohssokó**yi 'road', 6.18]

(m)otokís *nan* skin, hide [**otokí**si 'hide', 8.10]

(m)oyís *nin* dwelling [i'nió**óyis**a 'house of the dead', 5.1]

nááipisstsi *nan* cloth [**náíípisstsi**itapiima 'rag doll', 5.5]

náápi *nan* old man, creator, trickster; non-native,
Caucasian, white, English [**náápi**itapiiksi 'nonnative
people', 1.4; **Naapi**'powahsini 'English language', 1.4]

náápiikoan *nan* white man [**náápiikoan**ini '(who is) a
white man', 8.8; **náápiikoan**i 'white man', 8.9]

Naapí'powahsin** *nin* English language [lit. 'non-native
language', 1.4]

(n)aato *adt* holy, sacred [iik**áto**wa'piiwa 'it is very holy', 2.3;
naahkáísskssaw**aato**yi'tsiihpinnaana 'may we always
keep it holy', 2.4; aw**ááto**yistotsit 'bless it', 2.11]

niisííkopotto *nin* fourteen [**niisííkopotto**iitapiiyi 'they
were fourteen people', 3.31]

niisto *pro* I, me [see **iisto**]

niistonnaan *pro* we, us [see **iisto**]

(n)iit *adt* original, genuine, real [**niit**sí'powahsini 'real language', i.e. 'Blackfoot language', 1.1; kits**íít**si'powahsinnooni 'our Blackfoot language', 1.7]

(n)iitá'p *adt* really, truly [**niitá'p**o'totamá'piiwa 'it is really important', 1.1; aka**iita'p**omatapa'tsto'pa 'we've really started to lose it', 1.7; **niitá'p**iyikowa 'it was very hard', 4.8; o**niitá'p**ihkiitaanistsi 'her bannock' (lit. 'her real cooking'), 6.8]

niita'pihkiitaan** *nin* bannock (lit. real cooking) [o**niitá'pihkiitaan**istsi 'her bannock' (lit. 'her real cooking'), 6.8]

nioókska *adt* three [**nióókska**isskskoi'pi 'in grade three', 4.27]

(n)oohk *adt* please/COUNTEREXPECTATION [**noohk**áókamo'tsipo'tsit 'please keep it straight', 2.6; nááhkssa**woohk**ohtaiyissíniootspinnaana 'may we not be hit', 2.7; nááhk**oohk**aihtawa'psspinnaana 'may we have good fortune', 2.10]

Niitsí'powahsin** *nin* Blackfoot language [lit. 'real language', 1.1]

(oh)kana *adt* all [a**ohkaná**íítsi'poyio'pa 'we all spoke Blackfoot', 1.3; **kaná**ítapiiwa 'all people, everyone', 2.13; nitsít**ohkana**omahksiimayaawa 'I am the oldest of them all', 3.7]

ohkanoo *vai* assemble [áítsito'ta**ohkano**piiyi 'they would surround him', 4.16]

ohkiimaan *nan* wife [ot**ohkíímàan**a 'his wife', 3.5]

ohkin *nin* bone [**ohkín**a 'a bone', 5.5; **ohkín**i 'the bone', 5.13]

ohkit *adt* on top, upon [iitsít**ohkit**ssaipsstaiwayi 'then he stretched it (on)', 8.6]

ohkitópii *vai* ride on horseback [Aká**óhkitopii**wa 'Rides-Many-Horses' (name), 3.2; á**óhkitopii**wa 'he rode a horse', 3.18; ii**hkitópii**wa 'he rode on horseback', 8.9]

ohko *adt* contrary, undesirable, bad [ááhkssawa**ohko**iikiiyi 'may nothing bad happen to them', 2.9]

ohko *adt* have (the wherewithal) for [nááhkita**ohko**oyssinnaani 'so that we might have something to eat', 3.13; nááhkita**ohko**iipstópissinnaani 'so that we could have a place to live in', 3.13; nitsíta**ohko**oyihpinnaana 'we then had (some meat) to eat', 3.27; nitáísskssa**ohko**oyi'kookinnaana 'he always worked to get food for us', 4.7; nitááksika**o'hk**itsinikatawa 'I will stop talking about him, 4.28; maat**ohkóíí**si'takiwa 'she was not afraid of anything', 5.8]

ohkohtaa *vai* gather firewood [a**ohkohtáá**yaawa 'they would gather firewood', 7.5]

ohkoono *vta* find [máát**ohkoono**yiiwaatsi 'he could not find it', 8.10]

ohkot *vta* give to [nimáttayakiit**ohkok**kinnaana 'she also gave to each of us', 6.6; áíyaak**ohkot**siiwayi 'he was going to give it to', 8.8]

ohp *adt* with/ASSOCIATIVE [**iihp**ipó'tootspa 'we were placed (to)', 1.2; máátatt**ohp**aistawatawa 'they are no longer raised (to)', 1.6; p**ikímm**okinnaana 'be kind to us (for)', 2.14][4]

ohpapiiyihp *nar* relative [ním**ohpapiyihp**innaaniksi 'our relatives', 2.5]

ohpok *adt* with/ACCOMPANIMENT [nitsít**ohpok**oomawa 'I went with her', 5.9; nitáísskssa**ohpok**a'paissiimannaana 'we were always with her', 6.5]

ohpommaa *vai* buy [matta**ohpómmaa**wa 'he also bought', 7.8]

oht *adt* through, by, about/INSTRUMENT/SOURCE/ MEANS/CONTENT [ááhkstamm**oht**áíyissitapiiyio'pa 'let's just use it', 1.9; **Iiht**sipáítapiiyio'pi 'source of life, Creator, God', lit. 'the one through whom we live', 2.1; ní**moht**awaawahkaahpinnaani 'the path we walk', 2.6; nááhkssawo**ohkoht**aiyissíniootspinnaana 'may we not be hit', 2.7; nitáák**oht**si'poyi 'I will talk about', 3.2; **iiht**áíyika'po'takiwa 'he worked very hard', 3.13; ní**moht**aii'poyi 'I am talking about', 4.1; **iiht**ssáksiwa 'he left (in)', 4.27; ní**moht**siinapistotootspinnaaniaawa 'we were haunted by them', 5.16; **iiht**ssápawaasaii'niwa 'she was crying', 6.18; nitáák**oht**sitsiniki 'I am going to tell a story about', 8.1; nitsíík**oht**akayaapiaawa 'I saw (very) many of them', 8.2; íík**oht**akáíí'nikkiwaiksi 'he killed (very) many of them', 8.3; naaníst**oht**sitsiniki 'I tell a story about', 8.13][5]

4   See Frantz 2009: 92.
5   See Frantz 2009: 92–93.

ohtsimaa *vai* hear, read
[nitsíítamssok**ohtsímaa**hpinnaana 'we heard the news', 6.22]

ohtsissitapii *vai* use [ááhkstamm**ohtáíyissitapiiyi**o'pa 'let's just use it', 1.9]

okamo't *adt* right, straight, honest
[noohká**ókamo't**sipo'tsit 'please keep it straight', 2.6]

óki *und* (greeting), well [**óóki**, 3.1]

oko's *nar* child, offspring [**óko's**iksi 'his children', 3.6; **óko's**oaawaiksi 'their children', 3.31]

oksisawaaat *vta* visit [otó't**oksisawáaa**kkiksi 'those who came to visit him', 4.16

omaa *adt* yet, to the present time [see **iimaa**]

omááhkaa *vai* travel by means of horse or car, ride, drive [a'pá**ómaahka**nnaaniki 'when we travel about', 2.12; otáíí'tap**omaahkaa**ni 'he went there by horse', 8.9]

omahka *adt* whole [**omahká**ómahkimiini 'a whole big one', 8.4]

omahkimi *vai* be large [omahká**ómahkimi**ini 'a whole big one', 8.4]

omahksi *vai* be older [nitsítohkana**omahksi**imayaawa 'I am the oldest of them all', 3.7]

omahksísttsiiksiinaa *nan* rattlesnake
[**ómahksisttsííksiina**iksi 'rattlesnakes', 8.1, 8.12, 8.13; **ómahksisttsííksiinaa**wa 'rattlesnake', 8.11]

omatap *adt* begin, start [i**itomátap**aii'stamáttst
ohkatoomiaa 'then they began to teach', 1.4;
akaiita'**pomatap**a'tsto'pa 'we've really started to lose
it', 1.7; iitá**ómatap**iitsittsimaawa 'she would start to
cut up the meat', 3.25; otá**ó'matap**a'pao'takssi 'when
he started to work', 4.4]

omohp *adt* with/ASSOCIATIVE [see **ohp**]

omoht *adt* through, by, about/INSTRUMENT/SOURCE/
· MEANS/CONTENT [see **oht**]

omooni *vti* roll up [iit**omóóni**iwayi 'then he rolled it up', 8.7]

on *adt* swift [ááhk**on**iyika'kimato'pa 'let us (quickly) try
hard', 1.8]

oo *vai* go, walk [áákitsitap**oo**wa 'he went there', 4.18;
nimáttsitsitap**oo**hpinnaana 'we went there', 5.1, 5.3;
máátaitap**oo**waiksaawa 'they did not go there', 5.2;
itá'paisttok**oo**wa 'she was walking about there
noisily', 5.7; nitsítohpok**oo**mawa 'I went with her', 5.9;
nitsitssáó'tak**oo**hpinnaana 'we went around outside',
5.10; nitáísskssaitap**oo**hpinnaan 'we always went
there', 6.3; stap**o**íínnaaniki 'when we went there',
6.7; ásaakaist**oo**ka 'could you come over here for a
moment' 6.13]

oohtsi** *nin* location, direction [aahkiááp**oohtsi** 'at
home, back home', 3.23; sp**óóhtsi** 'up there', 5.7;
piw**óóhtsi** 'far away', 6.18; Pinááp**ohtsi** 'North End',
lit. 'eastward', 8.3]

ookóówa *nir* house, home [n**ookó**nnaanistsi 'our homes',
2.9; n**ookó**nnaani 'our house', 5.7; **okóówaa**yi 'her
house', 6.10, 8.9; n**ookó**nnaani 'our house', 7.9]

oostó(yi) *pro* he, him [see **iisto**]

oowatoo *vti* eat [nitááks**owato**'pinnaanistsi 'the things we eat', 2.11; nitsiikáíyaahs**owato**'pinnaani 'we very much liked to eat', 6.8]

ooyi *vai* eat [nááhkitaohk**ooy**ssinnaani 'so that we might have something to eat', 3.13; nááhkitohk**ooy**sinnaani 'so that we could have something to eat', 3.17; nitsítaohk**ooyi**hpinnaana 'we then had (some meat) to eat', 3.27]

ooyiistoto *vta* prepare a meal for [nimátta**ooyiistoto**okinnaana 'she also cooked for us', 6.7]

ooyi'ko *vta* provide food for [nitáísskssaohk**ooyi'ko**okinnaana 'he always worked to get food for us', 4.7]

opii *vai* sit, stay [nááhkitaohkoiipst**ópi**ssinnaani 'so that we could have a place to live (stay) in', 3.13; áítsito'taohkan**opii**yi 'they would surround him', 4.16]

ótapi'sin *nan* people [**ótapi'sin**a 'people', 5.2]

ota's *nar* horse [**óóta's**iksi 'his horses', 3.11]

oto *adt* go to do [**aóto**iikskimaawa 'he went to hunt', 3.17; iit**otóí**ssksinima'tsaawa 'then he went to school' (lit. 'then he went to be a student'), 4.26; nimáttsitsit**oto**yio'kaahpinnaana 'we went to sleep', 6.10]

ototaa *vai* make fire, add fuel to fire [ááksikaaka**ototaa**wa 'she would already be building a big fire', 3.24; áííta'**potottaa**yaawa 'they made fire', 7.3]

o'tak *adt* around [nitsitssá**ó'tak**oohpinnaana 'we went around outside', 5.10]

o'too *vai* arrive [otá**óótoo**hsaawa 'they arrived', 1.4; nááhkaii'taamaiss**ko'too**hpinnaana 'may we come back safe', 2.12; áó**ó'too**si 'when he came home', 3.24; i'**tó**ííyi 'when he arrived', 4.14; ot**ó'to**ksisawáaakkiksi 'those who came to visit him', 4.16]

o'totama'pii** *vii* be important, superior [niitá'p**o'totamá'pii**wa 'it is really important', 1.1]

o'tsi *vti* take [nitsítsit**o'tsii**hpinnaana 'we took it', 5.5; nitsít**o'tsii**hpi 'where had I taken it', 5.13]

paapó'sin *nin* lightning, battery, electricity [**paapó'sin**i 'electricity', 3.14, 5.12, 7.2]

pikkiáákio'ksisako(om) *nin* ground beef, hamburger [**opíkkiaakio'ksisakoom**istsi 'her hamburger', 6.8]

piksííksiinaa *nan* snake [**Piksííksiina**ikawahkoyi 'Snake Coulee', 8.3]

Pináápohtsi *nin* North End (lit. eastward) [**Pináápohtsi** 'North End', 8.3]

ponokáómitaa *nan* horse [**ponokáómita**i 'a horse', 6.6]

pookáá *nan* child [**pookáí**ksi 'children', 1.6]

sa *adt* out [nitsits**sáó'tak**oohpinnaana 'we went around outside', 5.10]

saaki *adt* still [ots**sááki**aii'nakstssi'si 'when he was still young', 4.24]

saipssta** *vta* stretch a hide for tanning
[iitsítohkits**saipssta**iwayi 'then he stretched it', 8.6]

saksi *vai* exit, leave [iihts**sáksi**wa 'he left', 4.27]

saommit *adt* shifty, furtive, 'here-and-there'
[**Sáóáómit**sikkanaayi 'Shining-Here-And-There'
(name), 3.4]

sap *adt* within [iihts**sáp**awaasaii'niwa 'she was crying', 6.18]

saw *adt* not/NEGATIVE [ááhks**saw**a'tsto'si
'may we not lose it', 1.1; 1.8;
nááhks**saw**oohkohtaiyissíniootspinnaana 'may we
not be hit', 2.7; ááhks**saw**aohkoiikiiyi 'may nothing
bad touch them', 2.9; otsíts**saw**omaitaihtsiihpi 'there
was not yet', 3.14; otsíts**saw**omawaakaitapísskohp
'there were not yet many places', 6.16][6]

sikóóhkotok *nin* coal [**sikóóhkotok**i 'coal', 7.8]

sipi *adt* night [**sipi**áána'kima'tsisi 'a night lantern', 5.8]

sipiáána'kimaa'tsis *nin* night lantern
[**sipiáána'kima'tsis**i 'a night lantern', 5.8]

sitsipssat *vta* speak to [máátai**sitsipssat**tsiiyíwaiksaawa
'they would not talk to each other', 4.21]

si'káán *nan* blanket [**si'káán**i 'a blanket', 4.19]

si'tsii *vii* smoke [iitái**si'tsii**maistsi 'then she smoked them', 3.26]

sok *adt* good, well [nááhks**sok**sistawatsimaahpinnaana
'may we raise (our children) well', 2.15;
áí**sok**itsinikiwa 'he was a good storyteller', 4.15]

---

6   See Frantz 2009: 84.

soka'pii *vii* be good [**soká'pii**yika 'good (thing)', 2.14]

soksisstaki** *vai* hang, be hung [áákits**soksístaki**o'pa 'it would be hung up', 4.19]

sook *adt* unexpected, suddenly [nitsíítams**sok**aníkkinnaana 'all of a sudden she told us', 6.12; nitsíítams**sok**ohtsímaahpinnaana 'we heard the news (suddenly)', 6.22; áíkkams**sook**sstonnatsstoyiwa 'it would suddenly get extremely cold', 7.1]

sopowahtsi'sat *vta* inquire, ask a question of [nitsíts**sopowahtsi'sak**ka 'he asked me', 5.13]

sopoya'pssi *vai* be thorough, meticulous [otsskáíí**sopoya'pssi** 'that he was very meticulous (organized)', 4.9]

ssamm *vta* look at [máátaakai**ssamm**otsiiyíwaiksaawa 'they would not be seeing each other', 4.20]

ssk *adt* back, return [nááhkaii'taamai**ssk**o'toohpinnaana 'may we come back safe', 2.12; a'páíyaak**ssk**sipohtootaawa 'bring them back!', 5.14; nitáíí'**ssk**sipohto'pinnaaniaawa 'we took them back, 5.15]

sska' *adt* greatly, extremely, very [máttai**skaii**'kimmiiwa 'he was (even) very kind to them', 3.11; ot**sskáíí**'sopoya'pssi 'that he was very meticulous (organized)', 4.9]

sskonáta'pssi *vai* be strong, industrious [ík**sskonata'pssi**wa 'he was very industrious (i.e. a very dependable worker)', 4.5]

ssksini *vti* know [nitsiikákai**ssksini**'pa 'I knew a lot about it', 3.15]

ssksinima'tsi *vta* teach [nitsít**ssksinima'ts**ookinnaana 'he then taught us', 4.11]

ssksino *vta* know [naníst**ssksino**awa 'I knew him', 4.6; nít**ssksino**awa, 'I knew him', 4.9]

ssp *adt* up, high [**sp**óóhtsi 'up there', 5.7]

sspommo *vta* help [i**sspómmo**okinnaana 'help us', 2.1; i**sspómmo**osi 'help them', 2.5; i**sspómmo**osa 'help (everyone)', 2.13]

sstonnat *adt* extremely, dangerous [áíkkamssook**sstonnat**sstoyiwa 'it would suddenly get extremely cold', 7.1]

sstoyii *vii* be cold, winter [áíkkamssooksstonnat**sstoyi**wa 'it would suddenly get extremely cold', 7.1; sawomáí**sstoyii**si 'before the cold weather came', 7.4; i**sstoyíí**si 'in the winter', 7.9]

sstoyisat* *vta* be shy toward [áí**sstoyisat**tsiiyaawa 'they avoided each other', 4.18]

stam *adt* just [ááhk**stam**mohtáíyissitapiiyio'pa 'let's just use it', 1.9]

sta'toksii *vti* split wood [ai**sta'toksíí**ma 'he split it', 7.7]

Tátsikiitapii* *nan* Standoff [**Tátsikiitapii**wa 'Standoff', 6.16]

(wa)ahkapohtoo* *vti* take home [nitsít**ahkapohtó**'pinnaaniaawa 'we took them home', 5.6]

(w)aahkiááp* *adt* back home [**aahkiááp**oohtsi 'at home, back home', 3.23]

(w)aaká *adt* many [maatsikakátt**aka**itapiiwa 'there are not very many people', 1.5; **Aká**óhkitopiiwa 'Rides-Many-Horses' (name), 3.2; iik**áka**itapiiyi 'they were very many people', 3.6; nitsiik**áka**issksini'pa 'I knew a lot about it', 3.15; ááksik**aaka**ototaawa 'she would already be building a big fire', 3.24; nitáít**aka**ohkayiimskookinnaana 'she would have a lot of dry meat for us', 3.28; nitsííkoht**aka**yaapiaawa 'I saw (very) many of them', 8.2; ííkoht**aká**íí'nikkiwaiksi 'he killed (very) many of them', 8.3]

(w)aaka(w)oo *vii* be many [ik**ákawo**yi 'they were many', 4.2]

waakissi *vai* get water [áá**waakissi**yaawa 'they hauled water', 7.3]

(w)aana'kimaa *vai* illuminate [iit**ána'kima** 'she then lit a lantern', 5.8]

waanii *vai* say [áísooka**waanii**wa 'he used to say', 4.25]

(w)aanist *vta* say to, tell [**ánist**ayini 's/he was called', 3.3, 3.4; nit**á'nist**ahsi 'when I told him', 5.14; nitsít**ani**kka 'he then told me', 5.14; nitsíítamssok**aní**kkinnaana 'all of a sudden she told us', 6.12; nitsít**ani**kkinnaana 'she then told us', 6.21]

waasai'ni *vai* cry [a**waasáíí'ni**wahka 'someone who is crying', 6.14, 6.17; iihtssápa**waasaii'ni**wa 'she was crying', 6.18]

waasani** *vai* mourn [á**waasani**wa 'she was mourning',
6.19]

waawahkaa *vai* walk, play
[nímohta**waawahkaa**hpinnaani 'the path we walk',
2.6]

waawa'ko* *vta* hunt, chase game [iita**wááwa'ko**yiiwa 'he
then chased it', 3.19]

(w)ai'stamáttsi *vta* teach, instruct
[nitáíí'tsini**áii'stamatts**ookinnaana 'she explained
everything to us', 6.4]

(w)ai'stamattsitohkatoo** *vti* teach, instruct
[iitomátap**aii'stamáttstohkatoo**miaa 'they began to
teach', 1.4]

(w)áyák *adt* both [it**ayak**sí'niyaiksi 'then they both died',
4.24; nimátt**ayak**iitohkokkinnaana 'she also gave to
each of us', 6.6]

(w)ayaksiksistsiko *vii* be moonlit
[iik**áyaksiksisstsiko**wa 'it was moonlight', 6.11]

(w)a'tstoo *vti* lose [ááhkss**awa'tsto**'si 'may we not lose it',
1.1; 1.8; akaiita'pomatap**a'tsto**'pa 'we've really started
to lose it', 1.7]

(y)ááhs *adt* good, pleasing, nice, kind
[iik**ááhs**itapiiwa 'he was a very kind person', 3.8;
nitsiik**áíyaahs**owato'pinnaani 'we very much liked
to eat', 6.8]

(y)áapi *vai* see [nitsíts**aapi**hpinnaani 'we saw', 5.11;
nitsííkohtak**ayaapi**aawa 'I saw (very) many of them',
8.2]

(y)iikano *vta* resemble [nitsítsiikanoannaana 'we take after him that way', 4.10]

(y)iinapistoto *vta* haunt [nímohtsiinapistotootspinnaaniaawa 'we were haunted by them', 5.16]

(y)iiso *vta* feed [ááksiisoyiiwaiksi 'he would feed them', 4.14]

(y)iitsittsimaa *vai* slice meat thinly for drying [iitáómatapiitsittsimaawa 'she would start to cut up the meat for drying', 3.25]

yissinio** *vta* catch [nááhkssawoohkohtaiyissíniootspinnaana 'may we not be hit (lit. 'caught')', 2.7]

yissitapii** *vai?* use [ááhkstammohtáíyissitapiiyio'pa 'let's just use it', 1.9; (variant of **ohtsissitapii?**)]

(y)isstsiiwo** *vta* listen [ísstsiiwoka 'listen!', 6.14]

yoohkimaa *vai* wait [áíkaitaiyoohkimaawa 'she would be waiting', 3.23]

(y)oohto *vta* hear [nitsítoohtowannaana 'then we heard it', 5.7; niníítomiaiyoohtowannaana 'we heard it distinctly', 6.17]

yo'kaa *vai* sleep [nimáttsitsitotoyio'kaahpinnaana 'we went to sleep', 6.10]

BRESCIA UNIVERSITY
COLLEGE LIBRARY